EVERY DAY
with Jesus
FOR GROWING CHRISTIANS

RELATIONSHIPS

BY SELWYN HUGHES

QUIET TIME

When I lift you,
my friend,
my arm grows stronger.
When I give to you,
my hand empties to receive.
When I walk you through
dark valleys,
my feet gain experience.
When I weep with you,
my eyes wash clear to see
compassion's holy bond.
When I lift you,
I am lifted.

"WHO NEEDS OTHERS?"
For Reading and Meditation: Ecclesiastes 4:1–12

"Two are better than one ... If one falls down, his friend can help him up." (vv. 9–10)

We are concentrating on the thought that God has designed us to need each other. One of the alarming trends in today's society is the increasing emphasis on independence, isolationism and "doing your own thing". Declaring a need is seen by many as a weakness, an open admission of failure, a flaw in one's character. Hence we see a spate of bestsellers hitting the secular market with titles like, *How To Be Your Own Best Friend*. Psychologists Newman and Berkowitz assert that in these books: "We are accountable only to ourselves for what happens to us in our lives."

DAMAGING ISOLATIONISM

The inevitable end of this "do your own thing" mentality is that people are held at a distance and sneeringly told: "Who needs you?" Read the backgrounds of those who are involved in this kind of approach to life and you will soon discover how damaging isolationism can be. Not so long ago, here in Britain, the town of Hungerford witnessed a massacre when a disturbed young man went berserk and gunned down a number of innocent people. The reports that came out some time afterwards showed him to be a man who spent most of his spare time in isolation from others.

This stress on isolation is completely opposite to the teaching of Scripture where the emphasis is always on involvement. Don't buy into the selfish, ego-centred lifestyle being suggested by many of today's leading writers – the consequences are bitter and inescapable. That's why the simple, profound counsel of Solomon which appears in our text today remains so needed – "Two are better than one."

An ego-centred lifestyle has bitter consequences.

Father, I see so clearly that today's emphasis on isolationism has a way of eclipsing the contrasting light of Scripture. Help me to take Your way in everything, no matter how plausible men's theories appear to be. In Jesus' Name. Amen.

"No Man is an Island"

For Reading and Meditation: I Corinthians 12:14–26

"The eye cannot say to the hand, 'I don't need you!' And the head cannot say to the feet, 'I don't need you!' " (v. 21)

We continue with the point we have been making: that God's purpose for our lives is not isolationism but loving involvement. Isolationism will not work. The seventeenth-century writer John Donne wrote these gripping and arresting words just seven days before his death: "No man is an island entire of itself: every man is a piece of the continent, a part of the main; if a clod be washed away by the sea, Europe is the less, as well as if a promontory were, as well as if a manor of thy friends or of thine own were; any man's death diminishes me, because I am involved in mankind; and therefore never send to know for whom the bell tolls; it tolls for thee."

OF EQUAL VALUE

These beautiful words are eclipsed only by the inspired writing of the apostle Paul in the passage before us today where he shows us the value of *every* single member in the Body of Christ. Isn't it interesting (and also disturbing) that so many Christians are committed more to the pastor or the leaders of a church than they are to each other? If I understand the thrust of what Paul is saying in this passage, our allegiance ought to be the same to everyone.

Twentieth-century hero-worshipping Christians have great difficulty in believing these words of the apostle Paul, but not until we see the value of each member of Christ's Body (rather than just those who are prominent in the Church) will we catch the idea of what is meant by loving involvement. Putting people on pedestals is not what the Church is all about. Everyone who belongs to Christ is expected to enter into loving involvement with everyone else who belongs to Christ – with no barriers or distinctions.

God's purpose for our lives is loving involvement.

Father, I am so thankful for Scripture which enables me always to see things from Your point of view. Help me to lean less on my understanding and more on Yours. In Christ's Name I ask it. Amen.

THE "I-CAN-DO-IT-ALL-MYSELF" ATTITUDE
For Reading and Meditation: Numbers 11:10–17

"... I will take of the Spirit that is on you and put the Spirit on them ..." (v. 17)

For one more day we must focus on the thought that we need one another. In the passage before us today we see that Moses had become a target for criticism and complaints of the people. Things had obviously got too much for him and he had begun to crack under the weight of responsibility. But God graciously relieved the pressure by bringing around him a group of seventy people to help him shoulder the burden he was carrying.

THE DOWNWARD SPIRAL

Strong leaders tend not to delegate responsibility as much as they should – a lesson I myself have had to learn. They often adopt an "I-can-do-it-all-myself" mentality and by so doing set themselves up for unnecessary stress. Add to this feelings of self-pity – feelings which often arise in the hearts of strong leaders, Elijah being only one example – and you have the breeding ground for extreme discouragement.

THE UPWARD CLIMB

How does God help us when we find ourselves spiralling down the tube of over-commitment? He brings someone alongside us to help pull us out of our rapid descent. Life gets pretty grim when there is no one to help. Bruce Larson says: "Life breaks down not so much because of the terrible things that happen to us, but because so few good things happen to us. A few words of encouragement, or a helping hand along the way can be like the little branches we climb to as we climb a mountain trail. No matter how steep the ascent, we can make it if from time to time someone gives us a helping hand." Fix it clearly in your mind – however much you are able to do, you cannot do everything by yourself. Moses, the great leader of Israel, needed the help of others – so do we.

However much you are able to do, you cannot do everything by yourself.

O Father, save me from this "I-can-do-it-all-myself" mentality. For I see that when I adopt this attitude, I am going against the grain of the universe. You have made me not to be independent but inter-dependent. Help me to be willing to let others help me. Amen

A TRANSFORMED HUSBAND

For Reading and Meditation: Romans 8:28–39

"... we are more than conquerors through him who loved us." (v. 37)

We continue reflecting on the idea that most of our problems in life arise from the fact that we do not love as we are loved. In one of my seminars I tell the story of a man I once counselled who told me that when he was a boy of twelve something happened to him that affected the course of his life. His father gave him a Christmas present which, when the boy unwrapped it, turned out not to be the train set he had expected – but a brick! As he looked at the "present" he had been given, the boy's father loomed over him and said: "That's all you're worth. You've hardly done a thing I've asked you over this past year. Perhaps this will teach you how to behave." From that traumatic experience the young boy made a decision: "I will never again trust anyone or get close to them, for they may disappoint me and let me down."

A FALSE STRATEGY

When he grew up and married, he found that after a few years his marriage got into serious trouble. It was clear that the strategy he had decided to follow: "Don't trust anyone or get close to them because you might get hurt," was destroying his marriage. I shared with him the truth that by holding on to the life strategy he had developed to prevent himself from feeling pain, he was violating the command to love his wife as Christ loved the Church (Ephesians 5:25).

Gradually he came to see that the reason why he feared rejection was because he did not feel deeply enough the strength and support of God's love. He repented of holding on to his wrong strategy, opened his being in a new way to receive God's love, and became a transformed person. And more – a transformed husband.

Receiving God's love can banish fear of rejection.

Father, I see how wonderfully Your love can drive out all my fears. Forgive me for so often depending on my ideas about how to make my life work instead of trusting Yours. This day, I open my being afresh to Your love. Love in me – and through me. In Jesus' Name. Amen.

THE SIN OF SELF-PROTECTION

For Reading and Meditation: Galatians 5:13–26

*"The acts of the sinful nature are obvious ...
selfish ambition ..." (vv. 19–20)*

The man I referred to yesterday had developed a strategy that kept his life together, but it was a strategy that violated the law of love. He was depending on his strategy to make his life work, not on the fact that in Christ he was secure and worthwhile. Only as he came to see where his security lay – in Christ's love for him – and to assimilate that into his being, was he able to minister to his wife without the fear of rejection.

THE "RELATIONSHIP-KILLER"

One of the main reasons why we are afraid to give ourselves to others is not, as many people think, because we are "shy by nature" but because we profoundly fear that others will withdraw from us and reject us. The fear of being hurt, let down, misunderstood, unappreciated, or rejected, keeps many of us from getting involved with the people God has put us in touch with. It is probably the biggest "relationship-killer" in the universe.

At the heart of this fear is a desire for self-protection. We cannot trust God's love enough to see us through the pain of being misunderstood or rejected, and so instead of moving towards someone in love we protect ourselves by holding back. We play safe, but at the same time violate the law of love. Larry Crabb says that self-protection is a category of sin that is not easily recognised in church life. Some have criticised him for coming up with a category of sin that is not mentioned in the Bible, but the term "self-protection" is simply a synonym for selfishness or self-centredness. When we fail to demonstrate love to others because we are afraid of their rejection, we are simply being selfish. We are depending on our own ideas about what works rather than His.

When we fail to demonstrate love to others because we fear their rejection, we are simply being selfish.

Father, I am so grateful that Your Holy Spirit has been given me to overcome all the works of the flesh. Let Your Spirit be at work in me today, helping me to resist the demands of my sinful nature and to receive the great inflow of Your love. Amen.

SELF VERSUS OTHER-CENTREDNESS

For Reading and Meditation: 1 Corinthians 10:23–33

"Nobody should seek his own good, but the good of others." (v. 24)

Yesterday we touched on the fact that self-protection (a synonym for selfishness) is a category of sin that is not often recognised in the Christian Church. When we are afraid to go towards others in loving involvement because we are afraid of the pain of possible rejection, in effect we are choosing to say to God: "I know You've told me I am to love others as You have loved me, but I'm not going to do it because it might bring me some personal pain." That is self-protection, which prefers withdrawal to involvement. And I have no hesitation in describing that as sin.

THE MARK OF THE CHRISTIAN

In Philippians 2:4 Paul exhorts us to look not only to our own interests, but also to the interests of others. One comment I have read on this verse says: "Clearly the dividing line between a life lived in the flesh and one empowered by the Spirit is self versus other-centredness. There is one source of energy behind every inter-personal act: either a priority interest in ourself, or a priority interest in others. The mark of the Christian is a quality of love that directs more energy towards others' concerns than towards one's own well being."

You will have noticed that many of your friends and families who are non-Christians are capable of great, even extraordinary, acts of kindness, but only a deeply committed Christian who experiences in his being the sweep of God's love can be more concerned with another's interests than his own. Very few Christians love like that. I certainly am very poor at it. Perhaps one of the chief reasons why the Church does not make the impact upon the world it should is because we love so poorly. We prefer the safety of self-protection to the risk of loving.

Only a deeply committed Christian can be more concerned with another's interests than his own.

O Father, help me, for I feel You calling me to challenges that I cannot climb up to in my own strength. Show me even more clearly that not only do You raise the standard high, but You also provide the power by which I can reach up to it. I am so thankful. Amen.

THE CENTRAL ISSUE

For Reading and Meditation: Proverbs 3:1–10

*"Trust in the Lord with all your heart and lean
not on your own understanding." (v. 5)*

We ended yesterday with the thought that far too often we prefer the safety of self-protection to the risk of loving. Let's face it, there are risks in loving others and becoming warmly involved in their lives. People can hurt. Their indifference, insensitivity, and sometimes their downright obnoxiousness, can cut deep into the human spirit.

PAIN FROM THE PAST

I am convinced, however, that the reason why we hurt so much when those whom we attempt to love reject us, is because the immediate hurt triggers off similar hurts from our past. Have you noticed that an unkind word from a friend, a snub by someone you respect, a sarcastic statement from a source you would least expect, can sometimes trigger off a reaction far more intense than the remark or action warrants? Why? Perhaps the words or action brought us close to the pain of profound disappointment that is deep within all of us – a pain that most of us desperately deny.

We have all been let down or hurt. There is not a person reading these lines who hasn't at some time been hurt or disappointed by others. Our usual response to these hurts is to make a commitment never to be hurt like that again. This commitment, if not faced and dealt with, becomes a barrier to a clear and open relationship with God and others. We try to love – but from a distance. We have to face the choice whether to run from the pain in self-protection or enter into the pain and trust God's love to carry us through. Self-protection or trust – this is the issue with which every one of us has to come to grips, not only in the matter of relationships, but in the entire field of Christian living.

We have to choose self-protection or trust in God's love.

My Father and my God, I see that my behaviour inevitably reflects one choice or the other – I either protect myself from further pain or trust Your love to carry me through. Show me the way to trust You more – dear Father. In Jesus' Name I ask it. Amen.

"BE NICE TO ME"

For Reading and Meditation: I Corinthians 3:10–23

"... the Day will bring it to light. It will be revealed with fire, and the fire will test the quality of each man's work." (v. 13)

We continue examining the fact that behind our relational style can be a commitment to self-interest that violates the command to love as we are loved. We were created by a God who desires us to trust His love so that we can freely love others and not protect ourselves from the pain of possible disappointment.

BEHIND THE FACADE

The reason we love so poorly is because we are afraid and unwilling to give up our commitment to self-protection. Behind a facade of friendliness can be a desire to please others so that they in turn will be kind to us and make us feel good. A friend of mine tells how she discovered behind her sweet smile and approachable manner a strategy that said, "Be nice to me because I can't stand being rejected." The person who is always cracking jokes may be doing so in order to avoid isolation. I have heard many comedians say that their careers developed out of a desire to keep people away from the deep loneliness they experience in their hearts. "A business efficiency," says Lawrence Crabb, "can keep people away from a tenderness that might be exploited. Shyness might be the means to keep us from ever looking foolish."

Of course, a commitment to self-protection does not lie behind *all* friendliness and concern — that would be taking things much too far. But a lot of it is — and we who are Christ's must be willing to examine ourselves to see whether our relational style is one designed to glorify God or glorify ourselves. In the final tribunal, when our lives are judged and the rewards given, the "kind" deeds we have done which were prompted by self-protection will be consigned to the flames, along with all other hypocrisies.

Our relational style glorifies either God or ourselves.

Father, Your Word tells me that if I judge myself I will not be judged (I Corinthians 11:31). Give me the courage I need to look at the things that may be going on within me, and help me deal with these things in a way that glorifies You. In Jesus' Name. Amen.

THE STEPS OF REPENTANCE
For Reading and Meditation: Hosea 14:1–3

*"Return ... to the Lord your God. Your
sins have been your downfall!" (v. 1)*

A s we have been seeing, once we understand how our
self-protective patterns work, we can enter into a fuller
appreciation of how God designed our lives to function and
how we miss the mark. Today we ask ourselves: How do we
repent of relational sin? Or, for that matter, any kind of sin?

RETURNING
The passage before us today shows us how it ought to be
done. *"Return to the Lord your God":* we have chosen to look
elsewhere for the energy to make our lives work; now we
must renounce that and make another choice – to transfer
our dependency to God.

RECOGNISING
"Take words with you" (v. 2): when we come to God we do
not stutter and stammer, wondering why we are there. We
must have a clear idea of what we are repenting of, and the
clearer our understanding, the deeper our repentance. The
Prodigal Son, you will remember, carefully rehearsed what
he would say to his father when he returned home: "I will
go back ... and say ... 'Father, I have sinned against heaven
and against you. I am no longer worthy to be called your
son' " (Luke 15:18–19).

RECEIVING
"Forgive all our sins" (v. 2): the change from wrongly relating to
rightly relating begins in receiving the forgiveness of God. We
cannot rid ourselves of sin; it is something that has to be forgiven.

RESPONDING
"Receive us graciously, that we may offer the fruit of our lips" (v. 2):
repentance involves throwing ourselves on the mercy of God
so that we may learn how to approach Him in true worship.
The thought here is: "Receive us so that we may rightly
worship." True worship flows out of an understanding that
the power to make our lives work is to be found in God
through Christ – and nowhere else.

*The clearer
our under-
standing of
sin, the
deeper our
repentance.*

**Gracious Father, You have built into Your Word such clarity and
direction. If I fail to follow it, it is not because it has not been
made clear; it has to be because I don't want it to be clear.
Help me to see – and follow. In Christ's Name. Amen.**

FURTHER STEPS TO REPENTANCE
For Reading and Meditation: Hosea 14:1–3

"Assyria cannot save us ..." (v. 3)

We continue looking at the passage in Hosea which spells out in detail the steps that are necessary to enter into a meaningful repentance. *"Assyria cannot save us; we will not mount war-horses":* when Israel was under threat from the surrounding nations, a pact with Assyria looked like a sensible precaution. But if Israel turned to Assyria for support, her dependency would not be fully on God. Assyria could not save Israel. If God failed to come through, Israel would be destroyed. Only when we see our lives in those terms can we understand what life is all about.

IDENTIFYING IDOLATRY
"We will never again say 'Our gods' to what our own hands have made" (v. 3): only when we see that the real issue underlying sin is idolatry (that is, choosing a visible god instead of the invisible God), will we see how our self-sufficiency violates the divine scheme of things. Our foolish attempts to rely on our own strategies as we relate to others must be seen for what they are – idolatry.

FINDING COMPASSION
"In you the fatherless find compassion" (v. 3): fatherless children are unprotected children, defenceless, and vulnerable to the point of helplessness. Repentance involves us in entering our disappointments and experiencing a sense of isolation and loneliness from which our souls would naturally shrink. Being willing to experience helplessness, however, enables us to see how desperately we need God and motivates us to turn to Him in utter dependency, finding, as we do, the reality of His compassion entering deep into our souls. Repentance may seem like a path that leads to death, but in the divine scheme of things it is the path that leads to life.

Repentance is the path that leads to life.

O God my Father, as I solemnly and sincerely take these steps of repentance, let them become the burning glass that gathers everything into one focus of love. I want to love like You. Then and then alone can I kindle Your love in others. Amen.

THE BENEFITS OF REPENTANCE

For Reading and Meditation: Hosea 14:4–9

"Who is wise? He will realise these things. Who is discerning? He will understand them." (v. 9)

Today we ask ourselves: What happens in the lives of those who know how to repent deeply? Repentance enables God to move into our lives with might and power.

FIVE FRUITS

The first thing that happens is that our waywardness is healed (v. 4). The compulsive desire we have to go astray and do our own thing is checked and brought under His control. The second thing is that our lives become spiritually refreshed: "I will be like the dew to Israel" (v. 5), and our roots go down further into the soil of God's love, giving us a deeper foundation and greater stability (v. 5). The third thing is that our lives gain an attractiveness that was not there before (v. 6). People sense we love them for their own sake, not for what they can do for us. Fourthly, this type of living encourages people to want to "dwell in our shade" (v. 7). They like to be near us for they become aware that in our company they are being ministered to – not manipulated. Fifthly, we learn that idolatry does not work and that the only fruitfulness that matters is the fruitfulness that comes from submission to God (v. 8).

"Who is wise?" asks Hosea. The answer is: the one who realises these things (v. 9). When we repent in the way Hosea describes in the first half of this chapter, we will experience the benefits he describes in the second half.

The challenge I have put before you over these past few days has been strong. I have walked this way myself and I know how disturbing it can be. But if repentance is to be deep enough to bring about changes at the core of our being, we must be willing to endure the challenge. No pain – no gain.

Repentance enables God to move into our lives with might and power.

Father, let the steps I have taken over these past few days remain in my understanding so that whenever I find myself moving in a direction away from You, I know how to return. Grant it – in Jesus' Name. Amen.

THE POWER OF A LOVING GROUP

For Reading and Meditation: Hebrews 3:12–19

"But encourage one another daily ..." (v. 13)

Yet another step we can take in order to develop our relationships with one another in the Christian Church is *to meet together in small groups for the purpose of giving and receiving feed-back.* How do we know how we are doing in the area of relationships if no one reflects to us how we come across to others? John Stott, in his book *One People,* says: "I do not think it is an exaggeration to say that small groups ... are indispensable for our growth into spiritual maturity."

EXAMINING TO ENLIGHTEN

One of the most transforming experiences in my life came after I sat for many hours with some fellow Christians examining each other's relational style. I learned that I would only share an opinion with others if I was sure it would not be disagreed with. I had to be always right. The group pointed out to me that this was defensive on my part – I was only willing to give those parts of myself that I thought others would be impressed with; thus they never saw the real "me" at all. I could have figured this out for myself, but it would have probably taken me years. The group lovingly brought this to my attention in hours.

> *We need each other's help to see the subterfuges and camouflages in our personalities.*

We really do need the help of one another to see the subterfuges and camouflages that go on in our personalities. Someone might say: "Why not trust the Holy Spirit or the Word of God to bring to light the things within us that need to be changed?" This is my answer: the Word of God shows us what we should be, the Holy Spirit shows us the work that has yet to be done, but our brothers and sisters in Christ can put their finger on the specific issues that need attention now.

O Father, I see how we Your people fail each other in not sharing with one another at a deeper level than we do. Lead me into a relationship such as the one I have read about today so that I can become more mature in the way I relate to others. For Christ's sake. Amen.

MAKING GOD MORE REAL TO OTHERS
For Reading and Meditation: I John 4:1–12

"No-one has ever seen God; but if we love one another, God lives in us and his love is made complete in us." (v. 12)

My final suggestion for developing good relationships is this – *focus on the fact that when you rightly relate to others you enable them to have a better understanding of God.* Every Christian knows that he or she is at all times wonderfully loved and deeply respected by God. This is an incontrovertible fact – nothing can be added to it and nothing can be taken away. There is, however, a lot we can do for one another to add to the *feelings* that underlie that fact.

EXPRESSING LOVE

Look at it like this: God is intangible and invisible. We, on the other hand, are both tangible and visible. We are able to see each other, touch each other, and hear each other. As physical beings we relate to one another in a way we do not relate to God and in a way God cannot relate to us. When you are feeling spiritually low or disconsolate and I move towards you with genuine care and concern, when I talk with you, smile with you or cry with you, when my entire body language demonstrates to you that I care, then, although those things cannot add to the fact that God loves you, they can add greatly to the *feelings* that go along with that fact.

God doesn't come to you and talk to you in an audible voice or put a warm hand on yours when you are in need of support – but I can. He has made me as a physical being and He has made you in the same way, too. And when I need support – you can give it to me. Together we can make the invisible God more real to each other and bring about in each other's lives an experiential awareness of what it means to be deeply loved by Him. Seeing this clearly, and entering into it fully, makes the task of rightly relating to others not just a duty but a delight.

Together we can make the invisible God more real to each other.

O God, the fact that I can bring home to my brothers and sisters a deeper understanding and a fuller enjoyment of what it means to be loved by You utterly overwhelms me. But I see it is true. Help me make You more real to someone today. In Christ's Name. Amen.

LIFE FOR EVERMORE

For Reading and Meditation: Psalm 133:1–3

"How good and pleasant it is when brothers live together in unity!" (v. 1)

We come now to our final day together, so let's gather up some of the threads of truth we have been developing and weave them together to form a final picture.

LOST JOY

Our biggest failures, we said, are failures in relationships and the most central is our failure to love as we are loved. To love means to move towards another person without self-protection, to esteem others greater than ourselves. Our Lord was the supreme example of this. For most of us, love is not the primary motivation of our lives – self-protection is. In trying to find our lives through manipulating others, we lose our ability to relate in ways that would bring us deep, eternal joy.

LOVE CHANGES EVERYTHING

The one saying that our Lord repeated more than any other invites us to lose our life in order to find it. But giving up self-protection is not easy, especially when what we are trying to protect is our natural desire to avoid increased pain. Why do we have this deep pain at the core of our being? It is there because of our arrogant belief that life is within our grasp. Unless we repent of that, we will continue for the rest of our lives in our attempts to manipulate God and others – instead of enjoying them. Only as we focus on how much we are loved by God, can we find the love that freely gives to others. People who are aware of how much they are deeply loved by God don't want anything from others – they simply love. Love really is the answer to good relationships. For love changes everything – and everyone.

> *People deeply aware of God's love don't want anything from others – they simply love.*

Gracious and loving Father, from this day forward help me to give out love in all my relationships. You took the initiative with me – help me take the initiative with others. And deepen my understanding of how to lose my life that I might find it again. In Christ's Name. Amen.